know your
PARAKEETS –
BUDGIES

Earl Schneider, editor

THE PET LIBRARY LTD

THE PET LIBRARY LTD ®

The Pet Library Ltd, subsidiary of Sternco Industries, Inc., 600 South Fourth Street, Harrison, N.J. Exclusive Canadian Distributor: Hartz Mountain Pet Supplies Limited, 1125 Talbot Street, St. Thomas, Ontario, Canada.

Exclusive United Kingdom Distributor: The Pet Library (London) Ltd, 30 Borough High Street, London S.E.1.

PRINTED IN THE NETHERLANDS

ISBN 0-87826-656-9

CONTENTS

Introduction

It's a toss-up today whether more dogs or more parakeets are being kept as pets. For centuries dogs held the record as man's favorite animal. But now in the '60s the parakeet is rapidly taking the lead. He has become Big Business! Perhaps as many as a million are bred and sold every year. Seed is carefully prepared, not only for his nutrition but for his epicurean palate. Furniture and toys are made just for him. Architects design his cages. Doctors prepare his remedies. Language records are pressed. Associations are formed. And books, like this, are written. All because America has fallen in love with this charming little bird.

And why not? There is no pet easier to care for and take to your heart. He's as beautiful as a rainbow! Spirited and playful! Entertaining! And most wonderful of all, he can be taught to talk!

Can you imagine a tiny little bird becoming a member of the family. Your keet will! He'll join you at coffee. He'll break in on your telephone conversations. He'll sit on your shoulder and watch TV. He'll ride on your dog's head. He'll admire himself in a mirror for hours. He loves company and company will love him!

This book has been prepared to tell you how to accomplish all these things.

Parakeet lore

For such a little bird, hardly bigger than an English sparrow, this graceful, beautifully colored member of the parrot family has been burdened with a lot of names. Scientists call him *Melopsittacus undulatus*. But the great variety of popular names bestowed on him over the years has led to endless confusion.

To list only a few, he is known as the Australian Shell, Zebra, Undulated or Warbling Grass Parakeet ("Keet" for short), and the Canary Parrot. In Great Britain and by many American hobbyists he is commonly called a Budgerigar, or "Budgie" for short. There is only one name he is not: a Love Bird, although for many years he was mistakenly called that. Today the name "Love Bird" is reserved for a stocky African bird, heavier than the Parakeet, with a short stubby tail.

The term "parakeet" is an anglicization of the French name for the bird: paroquette, meaning "little parrot". The descriptive names Zebra, Undulated, and Shell refer to the bird's distinctive markings: a striped or sea-shell pattern of black across its head, neck and wings. Budgerigar is an anglicization of the Australian bush-men's name for the bird "Betcherrygar" which can be roughly translated as "pretty good eating".

The parakeet's native home is Australia. There he groups with thousands of his own kind into large migratory flocks, traveling to water courses, and nesting twice a year, in the spring and again in the autumn. He lives off the wild grasses, their seeds, and the scrub vegetation of the dry grasslands. He was living there by the millions when first seen and described by two exploring English naturalists, Shaw and Gould. This was early in the nineteenth century when "as many as fifty thousand birds rose in green-and-yellow clouds".

It was not until 1840 that Englishmen were to see their first live parakeet; before then they had been exhibited only in museums as rare specimens "stuffed". In 1837 Gould wrote in a book all that he then knew about *Melopsittacus undulatus* (he was the one to give the bird its latin name), and ended up by saying ". . . of its nest, eggs, etc., nothing is known". How ironic it is to realize that within only a few generations even children would have first-hand knowledge of parakeets and their breeding habits.

Gould's brother-in-law, Charles Coxen, hand-reared these first birds and before long they were being bred successfully in captivity. It was then believed that they had to be kept in pairs, that one alone would pine away and die. It was for this reason they became known as "love birds", and because of it, the parakeet's amazing ability to mimic and talk took a long time to become known.

But even though parakeets could be bred in captivity, it was cheaper and easier to trap wild ones and ship them from Australia. So rapidly were the flocks being depleted that Australia finally had to pass a law forbidding their export. But this created no great problem. Parakeets bred under domesticated conditions are far superior in size and color and are healthier than their wild cousins. Aviaries soon began to appear all over Europe.

It wasn't long before an occasional mutation began to turn up. These were birds of different coloring. Soon breeders began to discover that they could produce many various-hued birds by selective mating. A light yellow appeared in 1875. Sky-blue ones appeared about ten years later. France created olive-green birds during the First World War. And the beautiful Cobalt-blues were first bred in 1920 by crossing Sky-blues with Olive-greens.

These Cobalts created a great fuss in Japan. In 1925, a Japanese Prince was intrigued by a pair of them he saw in England. He took them back to Japan as a gift to his sweetheart. This started a hysterical craze. Every Japanese had to give a pair of the beautiful blue birds to his beloved. English breeders were not able to keep up with the demand; in 1927 one pair sold for $1000. The craze continued until Japanese breeders got into the act, and bred the

Right to left: Olive Green Cock, Opaline Yellow Green Cock, Cobalt Cock, normal Green Cock and Australian Pied Hen.

Cobalts by the thousands. Soon with the help of a law forbidding any further imports, the prices dropped to somewhere within reason.

In the United States parakeet breeding developed slowly at first. As the hobby, or fad if you prefer, caught on, a tremendous demand for these birds soon developed. Yes, the Great American Boom was on its way and this lovely bird has established itself as a staple American pet.

Color varieties

The color of the wild parakeet as it exists in Australia is light green with a yellow head and black and yellowish seashell-like markings on the wings. In captivity, parakeets have been bred green, yellow, blue, white, gray, violet, and in every hue and combination of these colors. At this writing there are more than 70 *recognized* color varieties; there are many others which have not been recognized because they do not breed "true"—that is, their offspring do not appear to follow the accepted Mendelian laws of heredity. All these colors have sprung from the original green bird because of mutations (unexpected color variations) that were noted by breeders and then established by selective breeding according to the laws of Mendel.

All of the colors that have so far appeared are combinations of yellow and black pigment and a blue color effect which is not a true pigment. That is why we have yet to see our first red or pink parakeet. It is not impossible, however, that someday a red mutant will turn up. It happened after many years in the case of the canary when it was discovered that it could be successfully crossed with the South American Red Siskin. So far no parrot-like bird with red plumage and small enough to mate with a parakeet has been discovered. Some day it may happen.

Some of the newer colors are the Gray Wings, Cinnamons, Lutinos, Pink-eyed Albinos, Opalines, Buttercups, Yellow-faced Blues, Fallows, Apple-Greens, Violets and Mauves.

Apparently, however, the so-called "average" parakeet buyer prefers the "normal" colors—blues, greens, yellows. The pet department of a large department store made a survey and discovered that their customers' first choice was blue, green came second, and yellow third; all of the other colors were much poorer sellers.

4 Choosing your Parakeet

Don't dash to your pet department and buy the first cute bird you see. Choosing a parakeet is not difficult, but there are a few factors which should be taken into consideration—sex, color, age, health, for instance—and I suggest that before starting out to purchase your new pet you either commit the more important of these "do's and dont's" to memory or jot them down on a slip of paper to take along.

How many?

First of all, you must make up your mind if you want just one bird, a pair (male and female), two birds of the same sex, or enough to set you up in business as a breeder.

If you've never owned a parakeet before, let me suggest that you start out with one young bird less than three months old. He will be easier to tame and train because if he has no bird companion to talk to and play with he will devote all of his attention and affection to you. As for teaching a parakeet to talk, it is difficult to do if he has a bird companion.

If you are considering two birds because you have the mistaken idea that parakeets are "love birds" and will pine away in loneliness if not kept in pairs, forget it. You are going to provide all the companionship your bird needs.

If you are considering a *pair* with the thought in the back of your mind that eventually they will mate and bless your home with a lot of little keets, forget that too. A single pair of keets kept as pets in a cage, rarely breed. It can happen, and if you're lucky (or unlucky, depending upon your point of view) it may happen, but the odds are against it. Parakeets that have been tamed and trained do not make good breeders. They seem to lose all of their parental instincts and even when eggs are laid do not know how to incubate them or care for their young.

Parakeet breeding has developed in the United States to the point where there are many large scale breeders producing good quality birds at most reasonable prices. Our breeders have learned by now to choose their breeding stock carefully so that the birds you purchase at reasonable prices are of excellent quality. The average keet's lifespan is from twelve to fifteen years.

There are, however, a couple of ways to save money. Males are sometimes higher priced than females. This is because some people think, mistakenly, that males make the better talkers. They are wrong. A female makes an equally good pet, just as tameable, just as talkative. Finger-tamed pets usually cost more too because someone has taken the time to start their training. However any keet less than three months old can be quickly and easily tamed so buying a "hand-raised" pet is a needless luxury. Even adult birds, and they are the least expensive of all unless trained, can with patience eventually be tamed.

Nor should sex be a consideration unless you are planning to mate your pet. With some varieties the male's hue is darker than the female's, but the feathers of both are equally brilliant. Both can be trained to become expert talkers, do tricks; both will be equally loved. Young females are inclined to be more aggressive than males and more inquisitive. Yet they take longer to become acquainted and are noisier. So it's about six of one and half a dozen of the other.

Some say the aggressiveness of the baby female is useful when it comes to distinguishing the sexes. The female when first handled is more likely to bite harder than the young male. Also, baby females have a tendency to "cluck" softly when bothered.

Gray Pied Cock.

Yellow and Golden Pied Cock.

The cere

An accurate way of sexing an older bird is to observe its cere. This is the bridge of waxy flesh that surrounds the nostrils just above the beak. If the cere is bright blue, it indicates a male. If it is pink, pale blue or brown it indicates a female; at breeding age the female's cere becomes rough and dark brown.

With babies under six weeks old, this color difference is not so pronounced—all ceres are light blue—but the cere itself is apt to be plumper, brighter and more pronounced in the male.

Age

Choose a bird between six weeks and three months old, the younger the better (but never less than six weeks because they are then too young to leave their parents) if you want a bird that can be tamed, trained, and taught to talk.

A baby's age can be detected in several ways, one of which, the cere color, just discussed. All babies have light-blue ceres. Their eyes appear larger than older birds. This is because the iris of the eye and the pupil are both solid black. When the keet is about three months old the iris begins to lighten and by the time the bird is six months old, it has become gray. The pupil, however, remains dark for life.

The baby's beak is black too until it is six or seven weeks old; then this black begins to fade.

The easiest way of all to identify a young bird is by the striations or shell-like stripes which cover its neck and head. When the bird is between ten and twelve weeks old these stripes begin to slowly disappear and the "cap" becomes white on the various blue-hued birds, or a beautiful yellow on the green and yellow birds.

To sum up then, to be sure of getting a young bird, look for a keet between six weeks and three months old, with some black on the beak, solid black eyes and shell stripes on its forehead.

Color

No one color is better than another. There is no known relationship between color and intelligence; a green keet is not more tameable than a blue one. So choose the shade that appeals to you. You will undoubtedly have to pay more for what are called the "rares"—opalines, lutinos, albinos, etc.; less for the "normals"—cobalts, mauves, sky-blues and yellows. But under the feathers they are all the same, except for the albinos which have poorer vision.

Nor is there such a thing as a "strain of talkers" to be distinguished by color. Just select a bird that is brightly and fully feathered with a natural sheen.

Activity

Choose a lively bird who sits alertly proudly even, and who reacts to your movements. Avoid one that rests on its "elbows", lacks the long tail, and seems dull and unresponsive.

Do not choose a bird that cannot fly. However, many birds have had the feathers in one wing clipped to restrict flying. These will grow back. And do not clip them again. A bird who tries to fly, only to discover that he can't, quickly becomes timid and unsure of himself and turns into a poor pet.

You will, of course, not accept any bird with a hunched back, swellings, missing toes, ragged feathers, scaly feet, a deformed beak or legs, or watery eyes. Pay attention to the feathers around the vent. If they are missing or badly stained, a bowel disorder is indicated.

Today, good parakeets can be purchased at all kinds of stores that sell pets. Their demand has proven so universal that almost all pet departments keep a good and varied supply of parakeets on hand. We also believe that of all pets you can obtain for your home, a parakeet offers the most in terms of pleasure and enjoyment for the smallest possible cost.

5 Care and housing

Which comes first ... the parakeet or the cage? It is a moot question. In my opinion, the cage should be waiting, set up, all in order, when you bring your new pet home. Parakeets require big cages. Don't try to save money by purchasing a little one; instead think in terms of buying the largest cage possible. Your bird will be happier for it.

On the other hand, don't necessarily invest your money in a fancy, ornamental cage with all manner of ginger-bread decoration. Your bird's comfort is what you must consider; not the ornate appearance. Such cages are pretty to look at, but they are hard to keep clean. And your pet's health should be paramount in all your planning. He'll need plenty of flight room, conveniently placed perches and a swing, an easy way to get at food and water, etc.

Cages come in all sizes, styles and prices. You can purchase one for $3.95 in a dime store; you can buy a bigger one for from $10 to $25 in a departmental store or pet shop, or, if your taste runs in that direction, spend anywhere from $50 to $500 in an antique shop for a truly unusual one.

A Budgie which is raised with affection is eager to play with its owner.

Love.

"Watch the pretty birds."

A parakeet nest box: The scooped-out block simulates the rounded bottom of the hole in a tree which a budgie would use in nature. There are two sliding panels. The inner one, of glass, is for observation.

The Preferred Cage

Almost any metal cage is suitable for a parakeet, provided the bars are not too far apart and, as mentioned just previously, you can find them in almost any kind of a store and at any price that suits your desire.

Be assured your parakeet will thrive in almost any cage. The cost or aesthetic value of the cage is really for your taste.

There are a number of cages on the market designed especially for parakeets—their bars are horizontal rather than vertical, making it easier for the bird to climb. However any large bird cage, if the bars are no more than $\frac{1}{2}$ in apart, will do.

Let me repeat: the cage should be large enough so that the bird is not cramped. Otherwise, its tail feathers will constantly be brushing against the sides, and sticking out between the bars; they will be quickly frayed, leaving a dirty bedraggled bird. This is especially true if the bird is to be permanently confined, and not allowed to fly around the room.

Cages are usually made of metal although some of the more ornamental ones are of wood, bamboo, or woven wicker. These last, while pretty to look at, are impractical for a parakeet. Keets love to gnaw. A wooden or wicker cage will soon be a terrible sight to behold; more so if it was once painted. Wood, too, develops cracks and crevices in which pests can hide.

Metal cages may be either stainless steel or chromium-, zinc-, brass- or electro-plated. Stainless steel is the better but more expensive choice. All are easy to clean and will give years of service. But if the metal is cheaply painted, the birds will soon chip it off. So if you choose a painted metal cage, be sure that the paint is baked on. Such a cage is easier to keep clean and disinfected.

Check any new cage to make sure that no jagged-end wire is protruding. Clip it off or bend it in such a way that the bird cannot injure itself or catch its leg in a loop. Check it too for any paint globs that may have been left in corners; scrape them off with steel wool.

All new cages should be thoroughly washed with hot water and strong detergent to remove any traces of the acid wash they are given at the factory. But be sure the cage is thoroughly dry before the bird is put into it.

A plastic cage is recommended for those areas where there is a great deal of humidity and rust is a constant problem.

Another thing to check is the cage bars, either vertical or horizontal. They should be no more than $\frac{1}{2}$ in. apart because a keet can easily force his head through a larger opening, and then, if the bars tighten around his throat, strangle.

The cage bottom should slide in and out like a drawer. This is the easiest type to keep clean.

There should be a two-inch seed guard all around the bottom to keep seed hulls, grit, food, debris and feathers off the floor. Some cages come equipped with them; if yours does not, attachable plastic seed guards are available.

The cage door should be large enough for the keet to hop through easily, and it should have a double catch—one to fasten it open, one to fasten it closed securely so that the bird cannot open it with his beak.

If you can't afford a large cage, or if you want an extra flight cage for your pet, a fairly satisfactory one can be constructed from a large wooden box, the larger the better, but one at least two feet long and nine inches deep. Fit it with a hinged cover made of a picture-frame covered with $\frac{1}{2}$ in. wire mesh, making sure that no jagged ends of mesh protrude. Stand the box on its narrow end (for cage purposes its length becomes its height) drill holes on either side in which to fit two or more perches, and attachments for seed and water cups, and hang a swing from the top. Paint the inside with a non-toxic white enamel (the paint prepared especially for baby furniture) and the outside any color you prefer. Fit a metal

To illustrate adaptability of our parakeets. This pair raised two sets of youngsters while kept in an aviary of soft-billed birds. The cockbird is a Lutino, which is clear yellow with a red eye. The blue of the cere is not as pronounced in this color variety. The female is a Turquoise Blue Opaline.

tray into the bottom to make cleaning easier; or fashion a tray of aluminum foil.

If you buy a second-hand cage, or find an old one in the attic, scrub and disinfect it thoroughly, preferably by boiling it in water with Lysol, CN or one of the other strong disinfectants. If you should then decide to paint it (or to paint a new cage to match the color scheme) be sure to use non-toxic enamel. Apply the paint evenly, making sure there are no hardened globules when the paint dries. Never place a bird in a newly painted cage. Keep him in a temporary cage until you are absolutely sure that the paint is completely dry and odorless. The latex-base paints are always safest.

The cage should have a big hook or eye on its top so that it can be hung from a bracket, floor-stand, or from the ceiling, safe from other pets and mice, about five feet off the floor.

The cage's location should be carefully considered. Parakeets cannot tolerate drafts and with an open-sided cage the only way to prevent them is to choose a corner of a room that is draft-proof. Nor should the cage be hung in direct sunlight. If you do keep it near a window be double sure that, along with the sun, there is a constantly shaded area into which the bird can move.

You will probably want to keep your bird in a room where there is a lot of family activity, and that is good. But avoid the kitchen unless it is a very large one. The constant fluctuation of temperature due to cooking is bad for the bird and so is gas if you use that for cooking. Running hot water, boiling pots on the stove, and electrical appliances can also be a source of danger when your bird is out of its cage.

While you may change the location later, it is wise to keep the cage in one spot until the bird becomes used to it. The less often the cage is moved, the easier it will always be for your pet to find its way "home"

Seed cups

Newly purchased cages usually come equipped with seed cups. They are attached either to the inside or the outside of the cage. With the outside type, the keet must put his head through the bars to eat. At first he may not realize these cups are there so keep scattering his seed on the floor until he discovers them.

Always watch for the accumulation of husks in the seed dish. There is no nourishment in these and they must be discarded daily. Seed and water cups should be rinsed out once a day and washed in suds and rinsed in scalding water weekly.

Perches

Each cage should be fitted with at least three perches. Don't have them all of the same diameter. Different sized rounds help to rest and exercise the feet. One should be placed so the bird can stand on it within comfortable reach of his food and drink cups. Hardwood twigs can be substituted for perches occasionally. Keets enjoy chewing the bark. Most birds also enjoy a swing.

It is a good idea to have an extra set of perches to substitute for those that are being cleaned. Perches should never be washed. Washing softens the wood, making it easier to splinter. And if a bird is permitted to stand for any length of time on a damp perch, he will become rheumatic. Commercial wire perch scrapers are available; or you can use coarse sandpaper.

Gravel

As we pointed out when discussing cage-purchase, the bottom should be equipped with a removable drawer or tray to make cleaning easy. This tray should be covered with a layer of gravel, the commercially prepared kind especially for parakeets. This gravel should be discarded weekly when the tray is scrubbed.

About once every two weeks, the entire cage should be scrubbed and disinfected. But always make sure that the tray and the cage are thoroughly dry (either from being left in the sun or on a hot radiator) before returning the bird to them.

To make it easier, a mat of cedarized or gravel paper can be placed under the loose gravel to protect the tray.

Cuttlebone

You must always keep a piece of cuttlebone attached to the side of the cage. This is the dried shell of the squid or cuttlefish. It will help to keep your pet's beak in good condition, and it will serve as a needed health supplement—it contains calcium and other needed mineral salts. Fasten the bone securely to the cage with the soft side facing in, close to a perch. Replace it when the soft part is worn down.

Bathtubs

They do add to the keet's comfort in hot weather. Some keets like to take baths, some don't. If yours is one of the latter, don't force the issue. Instead, try putting seeds in the empty tub until he gets used to jumping in to eat them. Then later surprise him with a little water. Use a bird bathtub, or a small glass bowl with only a little tepid water in the bottom. Some owners add a little glycerine or borax to make the feathers glisten.

It is wiser to give the bird his bath in the morning; then he will be thoroughly dry by nightfall. Commercial "dry baths" are also available.

Some keets enjoy being sprayed with warm water from an atomizer. Others, when free, like nothing better than to fly under a running faucet. Be sure it's not hot water.

Toys

There is no end to the number of parakeet toys available. Don't clutter up your pet's cage with a lot of them. Give him a couple at a time, substitute two more, and alternate them from day to day. There are ladders to climb on, bells to ring, see-saws, ferris wheels, wagons, roly-polys. Plastic toys are easier to keep clean and less likely to be chewed.

Fortunately, parakeets have become so numerous that manufacturers have developed many different kinds of toys for these birds. We have mentioned merely a few that are available.

Many parakeet owners watch for new and original toys as they come on the market from time to time. It is surprising that a parakeet can be perfectly content with an older toy in his cage, but the moment a new one is given to him, he reacts almost like a child with a new baby doll or something different from what he, or she, has.

It is amusing to watch a parakeet with a new mirror. Immediately he rushes to greet his new friend. What chuckles and gurgles of delight! Surely the pleasure is contagious. Then cautiously he peeks in back of the mirror and, satisfied that there is no intruder, returns to the image. Perhaps he may try to feed the stranger by regurgitating a little food. This is perfectly normal.

The door of the cage should be removable or so hinged that it will stand open when the bird is out of the cage, allowing him to return whenever he chooses. Some cages have a flight-landing perch just outside the door to make entrance easier.

Cage covers

There are two schools of thought on this but the consensus is, if you start out using a cover then you must continue the practice. If your house temperature in winter drops suddenly at night, it is wise to use a cover. If the bird is kept in a room where there are lights and TV at night, or streetlights and passing cars are observable through a window, a cover will be needed in order for the bird to get its needed sleep.

If you're covering for warmth, use a heavy cover; if for darkness,

Budgies prefer to bathe under a water drip.

This baby's beak is undershot. Careful repeated trimming with nail nippers or a file can shorten the underbeak so that it will set in below the upper. In that case it will keep worn down naturally as the bird eats.

any light opaque fabric will do. Commercial cage covers are, of course, available.

Grooming

There are two things you may have to do for your pet: trim his toenails and his beak. Caged birds quickly develop over-long nails. Untrimmed, they curve back in such a way that the keet cannot grip his perch. With nail clippers or nail nippers, snip off the tips. Try to avoid the dark vein running down the inside; clip short of this. If there is some bleeding, do not be concerned; it will soon stop. A styptic pencil may be used to cauterize it. After the trimming, your bird will be much more spirited.

If your pet develops a misshapen or overgrown beak you will have to trim that too, or, if you are hesitant to attempt it, engage professional assistance. Use sharp straight nail clippers. Trimming will not hurt the bird although there may be a little blood.

Examine the underside of the upper mandible against the light. The dark core is the venous area; avoid cutting into it. The under-beak seldom needs trimming.

Wing clipping

This should not be done unless there is a real danger of your bird escaping or hurting himself. Sometimes in summer, with the constant opening and closing of screen doors, it is necessary to restrict the bird's flight. Only the secondaries need to be trimmed. Leave the last long four feathers on each wing uncut to keep the bird's appearance attractive. Both sides should be clipped evenly.

6 Feeding

One of the joys of keeping a parakeet is the ease with which it can be fed. The keet's basic diet is seed, supplemented with vegetable greens and a vitamin concentrate.

This basic parakeet seed diet is available in commercially mixed packages at most pet counters. The boxes themselves provide a convenient method of storing and will stack on a shelf the same as your regular grocery and food packages.

The manufacturers of commercial bird foods spend a great deal of time and money on nutritional research to ensure that your bird receives the correct seeds and in the proper proportions.

For the keeper of just one bird it is better to buy only a one-pound box of parakeet seed at a time; this way you are sure that the seed is fresh. Don't go in for large quantities of "bargain" seed because old dried-out seed or dirty seed can prove fatal. Seed should be kept exposed to fresh air so don't pour it from its cardboard box into an air-tight jar or tin box or keep it in the refrigerator.

The seed cup should be kept constantly filled. Never let it be empty; a bird deprived of seed for more than 24 hours will die. Remember, too, that your bird hulls each seed as he eats it, discarding the empty hull. These hulls collect in the seed cup. There have been many instances of keets starving to death because their owners thought the cups were filled. Each day blow the dry hulls off the top of the cup and add fresh seed. Once a week, throw out any seed left in the cup, wash and dry it thoroughly and refill with new seed.

Millet grains should be large, smooth in consistency and creamy white or light yellow. Canary seed should be shiny, plump and smooth. Small quantities of groats (hulled oats) and brown rice make good supplements. Oats (unhulled) should not be fed because the seeds are too hard to crack. While oats are fattening, baby birds need them, especially in cold weather, to maintain their body heat. Most keets consider groats great treats—like candy—so feed them accordingly.

Most millet is yellow millet; many breeders prefer the white or proso. Small red millet meant for finches is not digestible by keets but a few red millet seeds in the mix will do no harm.

Greens give your budgie his bright eyes and sleek appearance. They should be fed every other day, giving the bird only what he will eat at one "sitting", always removing any left-overs. After a few feedings you will be able to closely estimate the quantity. Most birds love greens. Because of this there is always the danger of their dining not wisely but too well on them, with resultant diarrhea. If this happens, discontinue green feeding for about a week.

Many owners choose to feed the greens by hand, making this part of their pet's taming and training. Others attach the greens to the side of the cage with a paper clip, removing them after an hour and throwing them away. Never allow greens to remain on the floor of the cage to become gritty and soiled. All greens and fruits should be thoroughly washed in luke warm water to remove every possible trace of pesticide which, even in a small lingering quantity, can prove fatal. Among the greens parakeets love are:

Clover	Beet tops	Grated carrot
Alfalfa	Celery tops	Celery stalk
Dandelions	Radish tops	Kale
Plantain	Carrot tops	Corn on the cob
Chickweed	Apple peel	

All should, of course, be freshly cut and washed thoroughly.

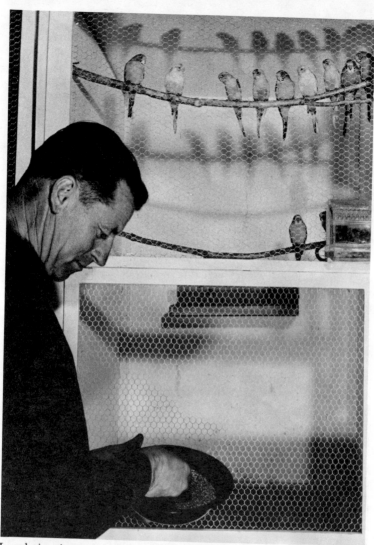

Lunch time in a commercial aviary. These are all babies which have been removed from their parents preparatory to sale. The absence of nest boxes shows that there is no breeding done in this cage.

Share and share alike."

Most keets also love lettuce and parsley. However these should be fed sparingly since, for most birds, they have a strong laxative effect. Sometimes too, these two favorites "spoil" keets for other greens which are even more nutritious.

Do not feed a newly purchased budgie greens during his first week with you. And if a keet has not been fed greens for some time, go easy on them.

Variety Adds Spice

Parakeets need a wide variety of different seeds and foods. Fortunately, these foods given as treats are readily available commercially packaged. These supplemental foods are absolutely necessary to young birds and also play a big part in the well-being of adult birds.

These commercially packaged parakeet treats and conditioning foods supply many additional vitamins, minerals and even cod liver oil. Most bird lovers have one or two of these supplementary foods in a treat dish in the bird's cage in addition to his regular bird food, at all times.

You will also find at your favorite pet counter egg yolk wafers. Since they need no refrigeration this is probably the most convenient method of supplying egg yolks to your bird.

Millet sprays give your parakeet the feeling of selecting these seeds as he would if he were flying outdoors. They are actually fun for him besides providing the added enjoyment from eating his seed in the "wild".

In nature parakeets are nomadic and migratory. They drift from place to place following the seasons. As these flocks of budgies wander they are constantly exposed to different types of food. Beggars can't be choosers; this is true of parakeets and people. So our little feathered friend must eat what he finds—different foods at different times and places. In our cage at home he must of course have his basic seed diet daily. However, varying the treats and supplements frequently, will add a more natural touch and increase his pleasure.

Contrary to popular belief animals, and this includes our little pet, cannot select from a variety set before him, those ingredients and the proper proportion to balance his diet. Like children, they have taste preferences. Given a choice between candy and basic food the child will always fill up on sweets and so will a budgie. Therefore it is wise to follow the manufacturers feeding directions carefully and avoid possible future troubles.

To digest their food, parakeets must have grit or gravel. There are special mixtures especially prepared for them, containing mineral salts and other digestive requirements: lime, shell, iron, bone, sulphur, charcoal, salt, sharp stone, etc.

Sometimes a young bird will not go down to the bottom of his cage for grit so, until you see him doing so, it is a good idea to keep grit in a small treat cup attached to the side of the cage.

Another dietary necessity is calcium. This is supplied by the cuttlebone which we mentioned in the section on cage accessories. If cuttlebone is not available, egg shells or a bit of plaster (mortar) picked out of rubble can be substituted. Never hang a cuttlebone on the side of the cage with wire or string. The keet while nibbling at it can work it loose and entangle himself in the hanger.

Refill the water cup daily. Water should always be fresh. Parakeets, however, do not drink a lot. They get much of their requirement from the greens. Which reminds me of something I should have, perhaps, mentioned earlier. Pots of live growing greens are available in pet shops, designed to fit the parakeet's cage. You merely add water and when the greens are about an inch high insert the unit in its holder. This is one way to be absolutely sure the greens are fresh. They do not, of course, take the place of all other greens. Variety is important.

7   The new arrival

You will, of course, bring your new pet home in a travelling cage well protected from drafts. When you get him there his new cage should be ready and waiting, prepared according to the instructions given under *Housing*.

Now I have a suggestion to make that you may not want to follow. Leave the new arrival in his cage for at least two weeks. Make no attempt to take him out, or to permit him to fly around the house. This does not mean that you cannot begin his hand-taming a day or two after his arrival, but do it in the cage. Let him become adjusted to his new quarters, and to feel safe and secure in them. It is highly important that the cage become firmly established in his mind as his "castle".

You will, of course, want to keep him in a spot where there is a lot of family activity (although not the kitchen), you will talk to him soothingly on every occasion, calling him by name, and you will see that his cage is kept scrupulously clean and that he is well and properly fed.

You must make sure that your new pet starts to eat. He will probably be "off his feed" for a day or so because of the strangeness of his situation. Have his seed cup full, but also spread some seed on

In about three days' time this baby will be ready for adoption. The band on his leg is a permanent identification. It also gives the year of his birth.

This close-up of a 5½-week-old Budgie shows all the characteristics which distinguish a baby: barred head, large solid black eye, and dark beak.

These two Budgies get along very well together although they're both males. Parakeets are always intrigued by glittering objects.

the floor. Many young keets will huddle on the cage floor the first few days but they will not be able to resist nibbling at the handy seed. If a bird does refuse to eat, it is a good idea to remove all the perches from the cage so he will be forced to sit on the floor among the seeds.

It is not a good idea, however, to put water on the floor of the cage because the baby will hop in it, spill it, get his feet wet and, perhaps, catch his death of cold.

If your baby parakeet has difficulty cracking seeds when he is on his own for the first time, help him by cracking them in advance with something like a rolling pin.

It is rarely necessary to do this for more than the first few days. When the black on the babies beak fades, he is fully capable of cracking his own seeds.

It is not wise to give a new bird greens immediately. Wait a few days at least, until he becomes better adjusted. If he then refuses them, dip them in water before feeding and, at the same time, remove the water cup. He must learn to like greens; his system needs the nutritional elements they furnish. At the same time, moist greens hanging in the cage will serve as a substitute for water.

For the first few nights see that the bird gets to bed early. Cover his cage or remove him to a darkened room as soon as he shows signs of drowsiness: his feathers will begin to fluff up and he will become inactive.

On the second day after his arrival you can begin the hand-taming which we now discuss.

8 Hand-taming

You should start finger-taming your new pet the day after you bring him home. This does not mean that he should be taken out of his cage. It is wiser to keep him caged for about two weeks so that he will become completely adjusted to his new home and regard it as a place of security. But hand-taming should begin immediately because your bird will be seeking new companionship now that he has been separated from his cage mates.

If he flutters wildly whenever you approach him, do not move away. He will think that he has driven you off and that is bad psychology. If he flutters, or crouches and cries for help, do not be alarmed. Stand there and talk to him soothingly, repeating his name over and over and telling him what a pretty bird he is. What you say isn't important—repeat the alphabet rhythmically if you can think of nothing else—how you say it, is. Your voice should always be gently reassuring.

The immediate object of hand-taming is to get your keet to sit on your finger whenever you offer it. However some believe in starting first with a "Tee" stick. This consists of two $\frac{1}{2}$ in. dowels joined together in the form of the letter "T", the handle about two feet long, the cross a few inches wide.

Open the door of the cage and slowly insert your finger (or the Tee) talking all the time. Stroke the keet's breast. Then, still moving very slowly, place your finger under its body where the legs are joined. Now give a command that you have previously decided on. It should consist of one word like "Up" coupled with the bird's name. Lift your finger gently, putting a slight pressure on the chest. Keep repeating the "Up, budgie" until the bird steps onto your finger in order to keep his balance. Hold still and keep talking. Keep it up for a minute or so and then slowly move your hand so that a perch pushes against the keet's breast. He will more than likely move on to the perch.

Never jerk your hand away if the bird flutters. Keep it in the cage until he quiets down, talking gently all the while, and then make another attempt. If the bird avoids your finger, follow him, repeating the command. He will soon come to realize that you mean no harm, and that your finger makes a very comfortable perch.

Taming periods should last ten or fifteen minutes, several times a day. End a period with the bird sitting on your finger; never when he flutters away, or cries. Stroke him before withdrawing.

Only after your bird accepts your finger on command should he be taken out of the cage. For the first venture out, wait until after dark. Then he won't try to fly through a closed window if he becomes startled. Fasten open the door of the cage. Command him to perch on your finger and slowly bring him out of the cage. Walk around the room talking to him smoothly for a few minutes and return him to his cage, closing the door. Repeat this several times; at night at first, and then during the day.

If the bird flies off your finger, don't make any startled movements. Remain frozen until he alights. Then go to him with extended finger, give the command, and return him to the cage. If he refuses, pick him up gently. If he flutters away again, don't chase after him noisily moving furniture. Wait until he lights and try again. If he lights on a high place like the top of a door or a curtain rod, use the Tee stick. If he continues to avoid you, have someone turn out the lights. He will not attempt to fly in the dark. Pick him up gently and return him to the cage. In the daytime a light piece of cloth can be dropped over him to assist in the retrieval.

The correct way to hold a bird is in the palm of the hand, with the thumb and first finger forming a circle around its neck, and the little finger around its tail. The second and third finger confine the body and legs. Hold the bird in this manner and scratch its head until it relaxes. Remember keets enjoy having their heads and throats stroked, so do this constantly during all its taming and training.

When he'll stay on your finger as you walk him around, hold your hand to your shoulder and try to get him to move on to it. A bit of his favorite treat placed there sometimes helps. Before long you will discover that your shoulder has become his favorite resting spot—either that or the top of your head; or the frame of your eyeglasses if you wear them.

House rules

Make it a rule not to let your bird out of his cage until you've made sure that no dangers exist. Winds and drafts can slam doors. Pilot lights on stoves can singe feathers. Large mirrors or windows can create illusions of open space for him to smack into. An open window or a hole in a screen is bound to be explored, inside—and out. Running water in a shower or faucet will attract and scald him if the water happens to be hot. Vacuum cleaners, air conditioners, fans, mixers, and toasters can all be dangerous weapons if your parakeet has the run of the house while they are being used.

9 Tricks

A young parakeet may be taught many tricks but the job is a tedious one requiring much time and patience, particularly if the bird's wings have not been clipped to prevent its flying away when it gets bored. Given this choice, I prefer to keep the wings unclipped and the bird's flight beauty intact. Instead I let my birds devise their own tricks, and they always do if given half a chance.

Playpens are available in pet shops. These are wooden, plastic or metal trays equipped with toy ladders, crossbars, bells, etc. They differ in price according to the elaborateness of their devices. After studying one, perhaps you would rather assemble your own. Remember, however, that strings, wires, loops and holes are dangerous so build your gymnasium with that thought in mind.

With such a playpen and with other of the many available parakeet toys your pet will constantly entertain you. All you have to do is sit back and relax. It is much more rewarding to tame your pet to come when called, to perch on your finger or shoulder of its own accord, and to talk. This last accomplishment far transcends any trick you may teach your bird.

10 Talking Parakeets

It is a mistaken idea that males make the better talkers. Females can be taught to talk too. What is important is to start with a young bird, the younger the better, and only one bird. If there is another bird, even a canary in the same house, the task can be somewhat more difficult. As soon as your new pet is finger-tame begin its training.

Training is a slow job, requiring patience. You cannot expect results for two or three months. Sometimes it takes a year. But once a bird has learned to repeat his first few words and phrases, there will be no stopping him. You will hear him repeating words and phrases he has overheard although they were never addressed to him. There are many cases on record where a parakeet has

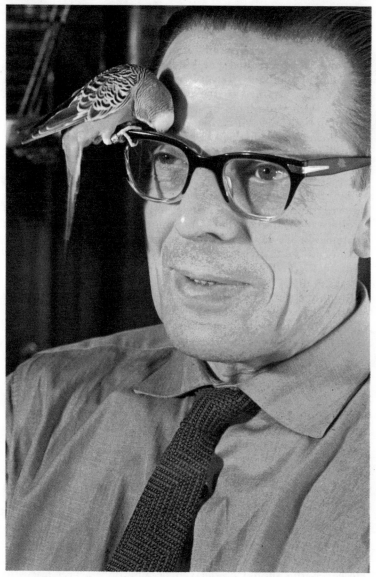

Completely unselfconscious, the pet Budgie is studying its own reflection in the glass.

repeated in the afternoon a phrase taught to him the first time that morning.

Your bird will learn nothing until it feels perfectly at ease with you, and has been treated with kindness. Its attachment to you and the sound of your voice are very important. That is why the person who is most attached to the bird should undertake its formal training. Others can help by constantly repeating the phrase the bird is supposed to learn, trying to use the same intonation, but that is all. Never let another person try to teach a new word while you are still working on another. It cannot be emphasized too strongly that the personality of the trainer plays the most important part in teaching a bird to talk.

It is probably best to start out by teaching the bird its name, or a short rhythmic phrase that includes its name—nothing so inane as 'Polly wants a cracker" but something along that line. Use a little imagination. It is not a bad idea to make the first phrase answer the usual questions that visitors commonly ask the bird. Answers like "I'm okay" or "Fine, how are you?" or "My name is Budgie . . . What's yours?"

Rhythmic phrases are probably better than one or two short words. They may take a little longer to learn at first, but the next phrase will come that much easier.

Do not say the words once or twice. Repeat them over and over each time you go near the cage, or when the keet is on your finger, or your shoulder. Some authorities believe that it is easier to teach a bird to talk if he is kept in his cage with the trainer standing to one side where the bird can hear but not see him. All agree that two of the best times for lessons are before the cage cover is removed in the morning and after it is placed on at night.

Training sessions should be for ten minutes at a time, at least twice a day. Your keet will not understand what it is to say. It learns by imitation. Wild parakeets do talk and imitate other bird calls. But the human voice has a lot to do with it. So the intonation is highly important. Speak slowly. quietly and distinctly, pronouncing all the syllables, and always in the same rhythmic tone. Repeat it not only during the regular training periods but every time you pass the cage, morning, noon and night.

Training a keet to whistle is easier than teaching him to talk. However, this should be delayed because once a keet learns to whistle he will keep it up incessantly and pay no attention to his speech lessons. Wait until he's learned a few words and sentences before you teach him to whistle and to sing. To teach him to whistle a tune, whistle only the opening bars at first. When he has mastered them, whistle them over but add the next few bars, etc., always repeating the whole tune before a new phrase is added. Keets can be taught to sing a song in this same fashion but it takes a long time.

There are on the market several parakeet talk-teaching records. Some people do record certain phrases on a tape recorder, repeating it over and over; the record method is certainly much more convenient. It is a good idea to repeat the record several times over at three or four different hours of the day.

During the training sessions, outside distractions should be avoided, for example, playing the radio or television at that time must be forbidden. Some people advise covering the cage with a light cloth during these sessions: not his night cover, but a separate piece of linen or muslin. This should be of a solid color as a pattern might be distracting. Removing his seed cup an hour or so before the lesson also seems to be helpful. If he is slightly hungry he is more alert and more aware of the recording. But, be very sure to replace the food immediately afterwards.

The average time it takes to teach a parakeet to talk varies with the individual bird. Many have spoken their first words in three months, many more in five months, even more in six months, and so on up to a year. Many trainers have felt like giving up in disgust one day only to go quietly into the bird's room and hear it talking to itself. Once a keet has fifteen or twenty words in his vocabulary, he will start adding new ones fast. Sometimes it takes only a couple of days for a good talker to learn a whole new sentence.

Once a bird has started talking at all, it can be taught progressively longer sentences. Always teach the entire sentence, not just parts of it. If the bird repeats it badly or slurs some words, don't work on the bad parts; instead repeat the entire sentence emphasizing those words clearly which are distorted or missing. Experiments have shown that the letters "m" "n" and "l" are difficult for the keet to pronounce; the letters "p" "t" and "k" easy. So take this into consideration when selecting your phrases.

Health care and first aid

Parakeets are hardy birds, highly adaptable to changing conditions. If properly fed and cared for, if the advice given in these pages is conscientiously followed, you have every reason to expect that your keet will continue in good health. However, accidents can happen, illness can strike, so it is wise to be prepared for some of the more common contingencies.

Do not attempt to treat a sick bird beyond these few "home remedy" suggestions. If they do not bring quick results, or if you have any reason to think that your keet may be seriously ill, consult

a veterinarian at once. That your bird is not well, you will recognize from his ruffled feathers, loss of appetite, listlessness, sometimes excessive thirst, discharge from eyes and nostrils, watery discoloured droppings and, perhaps, convulsions or shock.

Frequently a sick bird will respond to a simple change of food, a lighter diet, and a long period of rest.

Perhaps the first thing to do when you have a sick bird on your hands is to turn his cage into a "hospital". This assumes, of course, that you have only one bird. If you have two or more, you should isolate the sick bird at once. For this, you can use any small cage because his stay there will be only temporary. Cover three sides of it with heavy cloth and keep a shielded electric bulb close to it to provide added warmth. Try to keep an even temperature of about 85°F. A gentle laxative like milk of magnesia can be administered while you consider further measures. Use a medicine dropper to administer a few drops.

Many ailments will yield to modern antibiotics now available especially for birds. There is a prepared hulled millet seed that provides aureomycin and is given to the bird in place of his regular daily seed for a period of about fifteen days.

Antibiotics may be given in the drinking water. Dissolve one-fifth of the capsule's contents in a teaspoon of water. Put this medicated water in the bird's drink cup and give it no other water until it is consumed. Then, for the remainder of that day, give the keet fresh untreated water to drink. At night, remove the water cup so that the bird will be thirsty in the morning. At that time give him another teaspoonful of medicated water, and continue in this way until the bird recovers.

If a bird won't drink or eat, use a medicine dropper to dose him. Give him one drop at a time to make sure he doesn't choke on it, and always make sure that the medication is at the tip of the dropper in order not to force air into the bird. The bird can also be "force-fed" in this manner with honey diluted in water. About ten drops a day, one at a time, is enough. Put the tip of the dropper into the side of the mouth.

Invalid diet

If the patient will eat, feed him only easily digested foods: groats (hulled oats) or bread and milk with corn syrup or honey.

High Temperature

Normally a budgie's temperature is considerably higher than ours, about 105°F. That is why his little feet feel so warm when he perches on our finger. However on a particularly warm day, or in an overheated room he may feel the effects. The first sign will be his holding his wings slightly open and away from him. This is to increase the circulation of air around his body.

The remedy is simple—move him to a cooler area, or set a fan blowing close by, but not directly on the bird. If he is in the direct sunlight, shade him immediately.

Respiratory diseases

There are several but you won't be able to differentiate among them. They affect keets with symptoms much like those of the human cold: sneezing, mucus discharge, sinus inflammation, lethargy and shortness of breath, and wheezing. "Hospitalize" the bird and give it the antibiotic treatment as described above. Tempt the bird to eat or "force-feed" as described.

If antibiotics are not available, give four or five drops of whisky in a tablespoon of milk. If the droppings are loose and watery see the treatment discussed under *Diarrhea*.

Diarrhea

Sometimes this is a simple ailment in itself; at others it is the symptom of something more serious. The bird's normal droppings are semi-solid. If they become green and watery, and the feathers around the vent are badly soiled, begin treatment.

Stop feeding all greens and fruit. Hospitalize. Give a couple of drops several times a day of either Kaopectate, Pepto-bismol or milk of bismuth. The drops can be given either by a medicine dropper or by mixing them in with the feed.

Constipation

True constipation is unusual. What can happen is that the vent gets clogged with a matting of feces and feathers. This can be softened and removed with warm water and a cotton swab. If this is not the cause, then give a couple of drops of mineral oil or milk of magnesia or put a pinch of Epsom salts in the drinking water.

Vomit

It is instinctive for keets to regurgitate their food to feed the young. Sometimes they try to feed the "bird friends" they see in

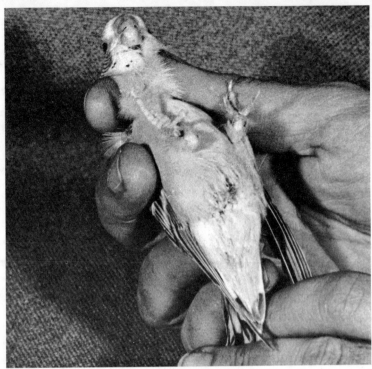

This poor bird is suffering from diarrhea as can be seen by the stained vent feathers.

mirrors. Do not be concerned unless it becomes frequent or is accompanied by other symptoms. If he throws shelled seed out of his crop and it has a bad smell, try a pinch of Epsom salts in the drinking water.

Crop binding

The crop is a small food storage reservoir that holds food until the gizzard is ready for it. Sometimes it becomes compacted with a solid mass of dry food, string, paper, etc. Mineral oil should be given, and then the crop should be gently kneaded. If this treatment fails, veterinary surgery is called for.

Egg binding

This, of course, occurs only in the female that cannot pass her eggs. We discuss it in the section on *Breeding*.

This keet is suffering from "French molt". The feathers molt prematurely so that it will never achieve a full feathering. The cause as well as the cure is not yet fully known. It is believed to be caused by a combination of poor diet and heredity. These birds are called "runners" or "creepers". Because of the constant molting their wing feathers never grew long enough to enable them to fly.

Apoplexy

On occasion a bird can appear to be in the best of health when it suddenly falls to the floor of the cage, struggles a little as if it had a broken wing, and dies. This is often the result of overeating and/or dietary deficiency, particularly lack of vitamin E which can be supplied in wheat-germ oil.

French molt

Loosely speaking, French molt is a kind of catch-all term used to designate more than one kind of feather ailment. Specifically, it designates an unnatural condition in which the bird is *constantly* molting, losing old feathers, growing new ones . . . so at no time does it appear sleek and fully feathered as it should. The quills are soft, pull out easily and, when opened, found filled with a dark foreign substance.

There are several theories, none of which have proven conclusive, regarding the cause of French Molt. Aviarists agree, however, that a liberal variety of supplementary and treat foods should be provided for these birds. It is recommended that treat foods, conditioning foods, egg yolk wafers, etc., especially be provided frequently.

At the same time, it is a good idea to spray such birds with a mite repellent once a week or so.

A fairly recent development is the use of long–lasting insect repellants. These are packaged in small plastic and metal containers. The seal is removed and the container hung on the cage. This emits an invisible, odorless insect repelling vapor for periods of up to three months.

Commercial preparations are available which can be added to his bath water. Not only will they help clean him, but act as a disinfectant also. Today, with our improved knowledge of nutrition and breeding French Molt is rarely seen.

Feather picking

Some birds, like children biting their finger nails, acquire the nervous habit of pulling out their own feathers and, on occasion, eating them. This should not be confused with the bird's normal habit of plucking out loose feathers. Bare spots can be soothed with vaseline. Try keeping the bird in a slightly cooler atmosphere. Give him something to occupy his mind—more flying time, perhaps. And, to be on the safe side, try the cures discussed under *French molt.*

Mites, feather lice

Cage sanitation is important. The keet with his everlasting preening quickly dislodges such pests, but it is up to you to keep the cage clean. Red mites may infect your bird. They hide in crevices or on the cage bottom and come out at night to attack him. If you suspect them, throw a piece of white cloth over the cage and check the next morning for tiny red spots. If found, scrub and rinse the cage in boiling water, disinfecting thoroughly.

Generally speaking, any dog and cat flea powder, or the aerosol sprays designed for the eradication of such pests, are satisfactory for birds. Be sure the powder you use does not contain DDT.

Internal parasites

These are rare among caged birds who have never been exposed. They include roundworms, tapeworms, flukes, and various other parasites. Only a vet can detect and prescribe for them. If you notice anything suspect in your pet's feces, take a sample to the vet for microscopic examination.

Oil duct obstruction

The parakeet preens his feathers with the oil he finds in a special gland on his back at the base of his tail. Sometimes the nipple of this gland becomes clogged. Massage it gently with a bit of cotton soaked in warm water and then use the *eye* of a large needle to probe out the dried oil.

Sore feet

Try to find the cause. It may be the roughness of a perch. If so, replace it immediately. Treat the feet with a daily bath of alcohol diluted with water, and then a zinc oxide anointment.

Urinary trouble

A urinary ailment is indicated if your pet drinks an excessive amount of water and its feces are mostly liquid. Treatment with aureomycin is frequently effective.

Accidents can happen

Parakeets seem to be accident-prone. If there is trouble around, they'll find it. Here are a few examples from a parakeet "Casualty List". One fell into a pot of hot soup; another hung himself on the cord of a window shade; a third broke his leg in the pulley of a clothesline. Many have been stepped on, or knocked off the top of a door when the wind slammed it shut. Never leave your pet out of his cage without supervision.

Broken bones

If at all possible, wrap a gauze bandage around the body to

Tail-pulling should be discouraged.

immobilize the bird and take him to the vet. If you feel competent enough to "do it yourself", follow these instructions.

If the wing is broken, fold the wing into its natural position with the bone ends touching and wind a one-inch strip of gauze about the body, and under the other wing, several times, holding it in place with strips of adhesive tape. Leave it on for about three weeks.

If a leg is broken, make a tiny plaster cast. Use surgeon's plaster, available in drug stores, or Johnson's Duo Adhesive. Have an assistant hold the leg outstretched with the bone ends touching. Apply a thin layer of plaster to the leg, and as it sets, press three half-lengths of flat toothpicks into it, and add a little more plaster. Now wind a narrow strip of gauze around the mass so that it sticks to the adhesive, and hold the bird in position until the cast sets. Allow it to remain in place for three weeks at least. At the end of that time, remove the cast carefully. Vinegar will help to dissolve the plaster.

Poison

Fast treatment is important. Give your pet a laxative—about four or five drops of milk of magnesia, drop by drop with a medicine dropper, works well because it is alkaline and an antidote for several acid poisons. Hydrogen peroxide is also good if you don't know what the poison is; dilute it half-and-half in water. If you do know the poison, administer a few drops of its known antidote diluted in water.

Paints, especially those containing lead or linseed oil, are a frequent cause of poisoning. So are mouse poison and the insecticides left on unwashed vegetables, or sprayed on house plants. After giving your pet first aid treatment, phone your vet, tell him what you think the poison is, and follow his instructions.

Wounds

Clip the feathers around the cut and open it to view. Swab it gently with peroxide. If the bleeding is excessive or the cut seems large, take your pet to the vet. Cuts heal in about eight days. Keep your bird warm and comfortable.

Broken feathers

There may come a time when you'll want to remove a broken tail or wing feather. Don't hesitate to pull it out. It will come painlessly with a firm tug. A new feather will begin to grow in. If the shaft is not pulled out, a new feather will not grow until the bird molts.

Shock

Your bird will lay prostrate on his side on the cage floor. Hold him in your cupped hands to warm his body. A drop or two of warm coffee, strong tea, or whisky can be administered with a medicine dropper, a drop at a time, to act as a stimulant.

Sudden chills, heat prostration

A sudden temperature change may give your bird a chill, or an over-heated room with poor ventilation may cause heat prostration.

Don't go from one extreme to the other. A chilled bird needs warmth, but not too much; an overheated bird needs to be cooled, but not suddenly. Gently warm the huddling, shivering bird in your hand; or, if it's too hot put it in an airy (but not drafty) area. Cool drinking water will also help to reduce its temperature.

13 Breeding

As we said in the opening section on *Choosing your parakeet*, budgies kept as pets, hand-tamed, trained, and allowed out of their cages to play, seldom make good breeders and usually you are wasting your time if you attempt to breed them.

This is not to say that breeding is difficult. To the contrary it is a hobby that even a child can carry on without any big expenditure of money; nor does it require a great deal of time. But you must start with a pair of birds that have been chosen for breeding purposes only. Then later, if you wish, the babies can be separated from the parents at an early age, raised in individual cages, hand-tamed while they are very young and sold at premium prices.

The parent birds should be fully mature, one year old or older, and be well nourished although not fat. They should be strong and active. The male's cere should be bright blue, the female's dark tan or brown.

The breeding cage, since there will be two birds living in it, should be as large as possible. As we pointed out in the section on *Housing*, metal cages are best; however, home-built cages of wood covered with wire mesh can be used if it is important to keep down costs. You cannot, however, economize on the nest box which you will have to add. These are sold in pet shops at varying prices. They are wooden boxes about five inches square and nine to eleven inches high. There is an entrance hole about two inches wide; and the top is hinged to give you easy access for observation and cleaning. There is a perch inside the box, the bottom of which is a hollowed out block of wood, a wooden "nest" whose diameter is about 4 inches and whose depth is about $\frac{3}{4}$ inch. The hollow is essential to keep the eggs from rolling around. It should be removable for easy cleaning. No nesting material is required. The female lays her eggs on the bare wood.

This nesting box should be either inside the large flight cage or it should be attached to the outside with its opening hole flush with a hole or door in the side of the larger cage. This cage will, of course, be equipped with the necessary accessories and perches described in the section on *Housing*. It should be placed in a quiet, secluded spot and *left there*. The birds will not breed if they are disturbed except for feeding and sanitation purposes.

Parakeets will mate at any time of the year; they do not have a definite breeding period. However, in the north, spring and summer are the best times, but in the extreme south, it is too warm in summer. There they should be bred during the winter. Not only do they know no season, they will breed constantly; quite often the female will start laying eggs again before her previous brood has left the nest.

No pair should be allowed to breed more than three times a year, however, as it will weaken the birds. As soon as the young can shift for themselves and have been removed to their individual cages for handraising, the nest box should be removed from the cage.

Some parakeets will mate soon after they are placed together in a cage and have discovered the nesting box. Others will take a long time. You must wait and let nature take its course. However it is fun to watch the male woo and win the female. Sometimes she will reject him violently; if she injures him it is better to separate the birds and secure either another male or another female.

You will know that the mating has been completed when the female begins to take a great deal of interest in inspecting the nest box, hopping in and out all the time. Soon she will start to remain inside throughout the day, rejoining her mate outside on a perch at night. Sometimes the male will feed her; sometimes she will come out to feed herself.

In about a week she will lay her first egg and then, every other day she will lay another, until a clutch of from 5 to 12 has been laid. The first egg will hatch in 18 days, and the others will follow on alternate days, until the entire clutch has been hatched. This means that there will be babies in all stages of growth in the nest at the same time; some almost fully feathered, others newly hatched and naked.

Egg binding

Sometimes an egg sticks in the cloaca and the female cannot pass it or any waste products or urine; toxemia soon sets in. You will not see her straining to pass the egg but you will see her sitting usually on the bottom of the cage, all ruffled and lethargic. Feel gently on both sides of the cloaca and you will sense the egg—if that is what is causing the trouble. Fill a smooth-pointed medicine dropper with mineral oil. Hold the bird carefully but firmly and gently insert the dropper between the cloaca and the egg; encircle the egg, squeezing out oil as you do so. Return the hen to the nest.

If she cannot pass the egg now with the lubrication, there is only one thing to do. Save her life by breaking the egg, letting its contents run out; crush the shell with a pair of tweezers and pull out the pieces. If you find another egg behind the first, wait and see if it can be passed naturally. If not, it will have to be destroyed as well. If the female suffers from egg binding a second time it is probably wise not to attempt to breed her again.

At one time it was believed that allowing the hen to raise only one or two youngsters in a nest would produce larger budgies. At first glance this would seem to be true judging by the relative size of this fledgling and its mother. However, when they reach maturity there is no appreciable difference in size between budgies reared alone and those reared in normal groups.

To the experienced eye Budgies take an individual character almost as soon as they hatch. The golden glow and the red eye indicate that this baby will be a Lutino.

The youngsters scrambling out of the nest are almost fully grown. The parents have started a new clutch.

Baby care

The baby birds require no special care or feeding. Usually the father takes care of it in a roundabout way: he feeds the mother and she, in turn, regurgitates the food for the babies. There is no harm in your opening the lid of the nest box to watch their progress even though the parents will appear to make a great fuss. They should be given fresh greens during this period.

The babies will foul the nest and it will have to be cleaned in spite of the parents' objections. Remove the babies to a temporary bowl and give the hollow block a good scouring with a stiff brush. Do not wash or wet it. Dampness might prove fatal.

As the young become fully feathered they should be taken from the nest—they will be hopping and flitting around by that time and eating on their own—and placed in individual cages if you intend to hand tame them, or in cages by sex, if you are going to raise them as breeders. Put their food on the floor of the cage for the first week or so, until they get used to eating it out of the feed cup. Their seed mixture should be hulled oats (groats), white millet and canary seed—this last in about 60% proportion because it is easier to crack.

If the female starts laying a second batch of eggs before all of her young are out of the nest, it is wise to remove them. Many females have been known to kill babies who got in the way while they were laying eggs. Budgies will continue to breed for about ten years; however they are at their best during the first three or four.

4 Genetics

To understand why parakeets have different colors, and how to breed for these particular colors, we must turn to the science of genetics and the laws of heredity. This natural law was first promulgated by the monk Gregor Mendel in 1865 but it did not become generally known and accepted until the early 1900s. Genetics—sometimes called Mendelism—is the study of how offspring inherit the features, traits and colors of their parents and grandparents.

It is sometimes difficult for those who have had no training in biology to understand Mendel's law. But explained in everyday English it is not too difficult and that is what I will attempt to do now.

The reproductive cell of the female is called an ovum or egg; that of the male, the sperm. When sperm penetrates ovum a new individual is conceived. Each parent contributes half of its hereditary genes. Genes are like tiny packages of coded information, linked together in a string of beads called a chromosome. Genes are always paired *except* when the ovum or sperm is being formed. Then the chromosome splits in two lengthwise, dividing the hereditary genes in half. Half of the mother's hereditary genes are in the ovum; half of the father's are in the sperm. The twain meet in the impregnated ovum and a baby is on its way. The newly formed chromosome contains the detailed blueprints of the baby's heredity—half from one parent, half from the other—but what if these halves differ? A baby can't be both tall and short, blue-eyed and brown-eyed.

Mendel noticed that when he crossed tall garden peas with dwarf peas, the offspring were not medium sized peas as one would suppose, but *all* were tall. The blueprints (genes) for Tall had taken precedence over the genes that blueprinted Dwarf: they *dominated* them, and that is how the term Dominant, now commonly used in genetics, originated. The weaker blueprint for size, Dwarf, receded into the background—it was *recessive*. It was still there; it just didn't show. It was, shall we say, dominated by its "better half".

This is why, many times, hereditary traits *appear* to skip a generation. They are there really; we just don't recognize them. We know this today. But naturalists didn't before Mendel came along. When he bred that second generation of peas (the ones that looked tall but came from tall and dwarf parents) he found that the new pea vines were *not* all Tall, that one out of every four was Dwarf. There were still, however, no medium sized pea vines in this third generation. Just Tall or Dwarf, nothing in between. When the Dwarfs of this third generation were bred together, their offspring were *all* Dwarfs. When the Talls were bred together, however, the expected didn't happen. Some of the Talls produced only Talls but some (the hybrids) produced Dwarfs. Mendel worked out the mathematics of it: 25% Dwarf; 75% Tall *but*—and a very important "but"—of that 75%, one-third would be dominantly Tall and the other two-thirds (50%) would look Tall but they would be carrying the recessive Dwarf genes.

Now let us forget about Mendel's peas and see what happens when we apply his findings to parakeets.

Let us substitute for the Tall pea, the normal Green color of the parakeet; and for the Dwarf pea, the normal Blue colored parakeet. Breeders now know from long experimentation that Green is dominant over all other parakeet colors, and that Blue is recessive to Green. The genes which dictate color in the Green bird are dominants; those which dictate the color of the Blue budgie are recessives. What happens when these genes meet?

For the purpose of explanation, let us call the dominant color *Solid Green*. Let us call the combination of dominant Green over recessive Blue *Hybrid Green*. Because Blue is recessive there can be no such thing as a hybrid Blue. We will call it *Pure Blue*.

Let us assume that each mating gives birth to eight baby parakeets. There are six possible combinations that can turn up amongst these eight.

These averages will not, of course, appear in any one particular mating. They have been derived by counting a great many matings and averaging them. Nor is it possible to tell the Solid Greens from the Hybrid Greens—they will all *look* the same. But the Solid Greens will give birth *only* to Solid Greens while the Hybrid Greens will throw *both* types of green as well as blue.

Three fine Pied Cocks. Two are called Yellow and Green. The third is Gray.

Gray Pied and Green and Yellow Pied. This picture shows the "spot" on the back of the Green and Yellow Pied. This spot is genetically linked to a strain of Pieds known as Australian Dominant and always appears with this strain.

1. If both parents are Solid Green, the eight children will be Solid Green.

2. If both parents are Pure Blue, the eight children will be Pure Blue.

3. If one parent is Solid Green and the other Pure Blue, the eight children will be Hybrid Green.

4. If both parents are Hybrid Green, of the eight children there will be two Solid Green, two Pure Blue, and four Hybrid Green.

5. If one parent is Solid Green and the other Hybrid Green, of the eight children there will be four Solid Green and four Hybrid Green.

6. If one parent is Pure Blue and the other Hybrid Green, of the eight children, four will be Pure Blue and four will be Hybrid Green.

Mutations

All this being true, you may rightfully ask, if each parent passes its hereditary traits on to its offspring with such mathematical precision, how can there ever be any new colors, sizes, and traits? What about evolution? The answer is that in some way still not known to science the genes for form or color are inexplicably changed in one parent, and then passed on to the children. Such an unaccounted-for change is called a *mutation* or, if it is a very dramatic change, a *sport*.

A mutation is produced when a gene is so changed that it results in an inheritable trait; a change that breeds true and can be passed on to its children and grandchildren.

Hybridization

Do not confuse mutation with hybridization. A hybridization is a change that results from mating but does not necessarily breed true. A hybrid is the offspring of two different species or varieties. Color variants are not considered separate varieties. They may be referred to as polymorphic variations. An example of hybridization in birds would be the so-called "Mule Canaries". These are the offspring of a Canary mated with a wild bird such as a linnet or a goldfinch.

To date we have not discovered any parakeet-like wild bird which will breed with our little budgie and produce viable off-spring. We use the word *hybrid* in describing color inheritance in parakeets for convenience. The proper scientific word for a bird with recessive genes which are masked by dominant genes is *heterozygous*; the bird which does not carry recessive genes is said to be *homozygous*.

If you would like comprehensive tables of all the possible mating combinations and expectations—a list far too long to be included in such a general book as this—and further material on the genetics of the parakeet I suggest you write to the American Budgerigar Society, 2619 East 12 Street, Indianapolis, Indiana, for a list of their publications.

5 Exhibiting

To the person who is considering breeding parakeets for exhibition, the best advice I can give is to "stop, look and listen". To be a successful exhibitor you must first be informed. You can study the standard for the ideal budgie, you can look at pictures and read books, but that is not enough. Familiarize yourself with budgie shows as a spectator, attending a number of them, before you actually enter your bird. Compare the winners with the standard and, if there is anything you don't understand, ask the judge or one of the old-timers you are sure to meet at any show.

Have a clear understanding of what is expected of you and your bird. Qualities like size, shape, condition, balance, deportment, shape of head, color, wing markings, etc., all are considered and rated on a point scale. Your bird will be judged on his behavior and poise as well as his ability to reveal his best points. A good bird who "stages" well often wins out over a better bird that does not exhibit itself to advantage. Your bird will be required to conduct himself with dignity while strangers—the judges—examine him minutely.

To achieve all this, requires the ultimate in patient breeding and training.

If you decide to go ahead with it, the first thing you will want to do is join a local budgerigar society, to find out when and where local shows will be held. I suggest that you write to the American Budgerigar Society, 2619 East 12 Street, Indianapolis, Indiana, for information about groups in your locality.

Opaline Gray Green Cock.

This is a very well bred Olive Green Cock. To be a show winner he should have a more erect posture. He is an excellent father and five of his offspring have won major show awards.

At a Budgerigar show the judge uses his wand to prod the entrants into position and to check their stance.

16 Standard for the ideal Budgerigar

Condition: This is essential. If a bird is not in condition, it should never be considered.

Type: Gracefully tapered from nape of neck to tip of tail, with an approximately straight back line, and a rather deep curved chest. The bird should be perfectly balanced and convey the impression of being well and evenly proportioned.

Length: The ideal length is $8\frac{1}{2}$ inches from crown of the head to the tip of the tail. American judges frequently consider the ideal bird to be a little smaller than this.

Head: Large, round, wide and symmetrical when viewed from any angle; curvature of skull commencing at cere, to lift outward and upward, continuing in one graceful sweep over the top and base of head.

Beak: Set well into face.

Eyes: Bold and bright, positioned well away from front, top and back skull.

Neck: Short and wide when viewed from either side or front.

Wings: Well braced, carried just above the cushion of the tail and not crossed. The ideal wing length is $3\frac{3}{4}$ inches from the butt to the tip of the longest primary flight.

Tail: To be straight and tight with two long tail feathers.

Position: Steady on the perch at an angle of 30 degrees from the vertical, looking fearless and natural.

Mask and spots: Mask to be clear, deep and wide, ornamented by six evenly spaced large round throat spots, the outer two being partially covered at the base of the cheek patches, the size of the spots to be in proportion to the rest of the make-up of the bird. Spots can be either too large or too small.

Legs and feet: Legs should be straight and strong, with two front and two rear toes and claws firmly gripping the perch.

Markings: Wavy markings on cheek, head, neck, back and wings to stand out clearly.

Color: Clear and level and of an even shade.

When judged, the total point scoring (except for opalines, cinnamons, albinos, and a few rare varieties) adds up to a hundred which means perfection and is scaled like this:

This Blue Normal Cock has won eleven premium awards. A beautiful bird and a great showman.

SCALE OF POINTS

Size, Shape, Condition, Balance	30
Deportment and Wing Carriage	15
Size and Shape of Head	20
Color	15
Mask and Spots	15
Wing Markings	5
Total	**100**

A Rainbow Hen. The type is poor, but the colors are enchanting. Genetically it is quite an accomplishment to produce all these colors on one bird.

A bird market in Europe. The quality of the Budgies in this cage is surprisingly good, considering the conditions.